THE WORLD OF
JAZZ

TEXT BY
GIUSEPPE VIGNA

ILLUSTRATIONS BY
STUDIO BONI·PIERI·CRITONE

W
FRANKLIN WATTS
LONDON•SYDNEY

DoGi

This edition
first published in
Great Britain in 2002

Franklin Watts
96 Leonard Street
London EC2A 4XD

Franklin Watts Australia
45-51 Huntley Street
Alexandria NSW 2015

ISBN 0 7496 4765 5 (pbk)

A CIP catalogue record
for this book
is available from
the British Library

English translation ©
Copyright 1999
by Barron's Educational
Series, Inc.

Original edition © 1998 by
DoGi spa, Florence, Italy

Printed in Italy

All rights reserved.

Originally published as
Il jazz e la sua storia

Written by
Guiseppe Vigna
with revisions by
Leonardo Bonechi

Graphic design:
Francesco Lo Bello

Illustrations:
Studio Boni-Pieri-Critone

Art director:
Sebastiano Ranchetti

Page make-up:
Katherine Carson Forden
Sebastiano Ranchetti

Picture research:
Katherine Carson Forden

Editor:
Andrea Bachini

English translation by:
Anna Maria Salmeri
Pherson

HOW TO READ THIS BOOK

Every facing page is a chapter on the social, cultural and historical background, the main personalities, the instruments or the great moments in the history of jazz. The text on the left at the top of the page (1) and *the large central illustration present the main theme. The other elements on the page—photographs, reproductions of contemporary prints and portraits— provide additional information.*

ACKNOWLEDGMENTS

ABBREVIATIONS: t: top / b: bottom / c: centre / r: right / l: left

ILLUSTRATIONS: The illustrations in this volume are new and original. They have been specially commissioned by DoGi spa, which owns the copyright. DESIGN by Studio Boni-Pieri-Critone, Lucia Mattioli, Armando Ponzecchi, and Alessandro Rabatti
COVER by Luciano Crovato and Gianni Mazzoleni (centre) and Luigi Critone
BACK COVER by Luigi Critone

LIST OF REPRODUCTIONS:
DoGi spa has done its best to discover possible rights of third parties. We apologize for any omissions or mistakes that might have occurred, and will be pleased to introduce the appropriate corrections in later editions of this book. We would like to thank the Library of North American History and Literature at the History Department of the University of Florence.

(The works reproduced in their integrity are followed by the consonant t; those partially reproduced are followed by the consonant p.)
6l Anonymous, *View of French Cape and the Boat Le Marie Seraphique of Nantes,* end of 1700, watercolour (NANTES, MUSÉE DES SALORGES) p; **6tr** Anonymous, *The Slave Trade,* engraving (IGDA-RIZZOLI, MILAN) t; **7d** E. Jahn, *The First Battle of Bull Run in the Civil War,* print from Eslon's Civil War (PHOTO MARY EVANS PICTURE LIBRARY, LONDON) t; **8tl** *A Cotton Flower,* coloured engraving (PHOTO MARY EVANS PICTURE LIBRARY, LONDON) t; **11tr** *A Troupe of Minstrels,* early 1900s (ARCHIVE DOGI, FLORENCE) p; **12t** *Robert Johnson*

(DIME STORE PHOTO) p; **13tl** *Bessie Smith* (ARCHIVE NORDISK) p; **13tr** *Sheet Music of Maple Leaf Rag* by Scott Joplin (ARCHIVE ALVAR) t; **14bl** *A Riverboat,* colored lithograph (ARCHIVE CURRIER & IVES) t; **14tr** *King Oliver* (IGDA, MILAN) t; **15tr** *A Street in Storyville* (ARCHIVE MAX JONES) p; **16tl** *Louis Armstrong* (RCS-IGDA, MILAN) p; **17tr** *Bix Beiderbecke* (ARCHIVE MAX JONES) t; **18tl** *Jelly Roll Morton* (ARCHIVE ALVAR) p; **18bl** Cover of the edition *Hot Jazz* by Jelly Roll Morton (PHOTO FEDERICO GONZALES) p; **19tr** *Fletcher Henderson* (FBA, MILAN) p; **20t** *Alcoholic beverages confiscated at Luigi's,* January 1923 (PHOTO MUSEUM OF THE CITY OF NEW YORK, NEW YORK) t; **21tr** *George Gershwin* (PHOTO MICHAEL OCHS ARCHIVES/REDFERNS, LONDON) t; **21br** *F. Scott Fitzgerald,* circa 1925 (SNAP PHOTO/JR/GRAZIA NERI, MILAN) p; **22t** *Cotton Club* (PHOTO JAZZ MUSIC; RUSCONI PUBLISHER) t; **23tl** *Cab Calloway* (PHOTO ROLF DAHLGREN) p; **23tc** *Fats Waller* (FRANK DRIGGS COLLECTION) t; **23tr** *Duke Ellington* (FRANK DRIGGS COLLECTION) p; **24l** *Django Reinhardt* (FRANK DRIGGS COLLECTION) p; **25tr** *Sidney Bechet* (PHOTO BERYLE BEMOEN) p; **26t** *Count Basie* (ARCHIVE BARAZZETTA) t; **27tl** *Lester Young* (PHOTO FBS, MILAN) p; **27tc** *Roy Eldridge* (FRANK DRIGGS COLLECTION) p; **27tr** Cover by Billie Holiday at *Jazz at the Philharmonic* (CLEF RECORDS) t; **27br** *Art Tatum* (FRANK DRIGGS COLLECTION) p; **29tr** *Benny Goodman* (IGDA, MILAN) p; **29b** *Carnegie Hall,* engraving, Alfred Scott Publisher (CARNEGIE HALL ARCHIVES, NEW YORK) t; **30l** *Baby Dodds* (PHOTO JAZZ MUSIC; RUSCONI PUBLISHER) p; **31tr** *Kenny Clarke* (PHOTO HERMAN LEONARD) p; **31br** *Elvin Jones* (PHOTO BRIAN FOSKETT) p;

31bl *Jo Jones* (PHOTO VERYL C. OAKLAND) p; **32t** *Coleman Hawkins* (FBS, MILAN) p; **33tr** *Cassandra Wilson* (PHOTO EBET ROBERTS/REDFERNS, LONDON) t; **34tl** *Billie Holiday* (PHOTO WILLIAM GOTTLIEB/REDFERNS, LONDON) p; **34tr** *Carmen McRae* (PHOTO JAZZ MUSIC, RUSCONI PUBLISHER) t; **35tc** *Frank Sinatra* (RCS-IGDA, MILAN) p; **35tr** *Louis Armstrong* (ARCHIVE RBA-POGGI, MILAN) p; **36t** *Glenn Miller* (PHOTO GIAN CARLO RONCAGLIERE) p; **37tl** *The Allies' Victory,* 1943, Naples (PHOTO ROBERT CAPA/AGENZIA CONTRASTO, ROME) t; **37tr** Original V-Disc Collection Cover (RUSCONI PUBLISHER) t; **38tl** *Charlie Parker* (ARCHIVE RBA, MILAN) p; **38tr** *Charlie Christian* (FRANK DRIGGS COLLECTION) p; **39tr** *Dizzy Gillespie* (FBS, MILAN) p; **39b** *Bud Powell* (PHOTO VAL WILMER) p; **40tl** *Elvis Presley* (ARCHIVE CURCIO, ROME) p; **40b** *Keith Richards* (ARCHIVE CURCIO, ROME) p; **41tl** *Ray Charles* (PHOTO DAVID REDFERN/REDFERNS, LONDON) t; **41tc** *James Brown* (PHOTO DAVID REDFERN/REDFERNS, LONDON) p; **42t** *The Quartet of Gerry Mulligan and Chet Baker* (ARCHIVE RBA, MILAN) p; **42bl** *The Modern Jazz Quartet* (PHOTO HERMAN LEONARD) p; **43tr** *Lennie Tristano* (PHOTO BOB PARENT) t; **44tl** *Collection of Records* (PRIVATE COLLECTION, FLORENCE) t; **47tr** Cover of the Edition *Ellington at Newport* (CBS JAZZ MASTERPIECES) t; **48tl** *Sonny Rollins* (MOSAIC IMAGES) p; **48c** *Art Blakey* (FBS, MILAN) p; **48b** *Bill Evans* (PHOTO DAVID REDFERN/REDFERNS, LONDON) t; **49tr** *Thelonious Monk* (PHOTO BRIAN FOSKETT) p; **50tl** *Charles Mingus* (PHOTO GIANCARLO RONCAGLIA) p; **51** Cover of the edition *We Insist! Max Roach's Freedom Now Suite*

(AMIGO MUSIKPRODUKTION; PHOTO HUGH BELL) t; **52tl** *Ornette Coleman* (PHOTO ELIGIO PAONI/AGENZIA CONTRASTO, ROME) t; **52c** *Eric Dolphy* (IGDA, MILAN) p; **52tr** *Archie Shepp* (CHARLIE RECORDES LTD, LONDON) p; **53tl** *Sun Ra* (PHOTO GENNARO CILENTO) p; **53tc** *Malcolm X* (PHOTO EVE ARNOLD/MAGNUM/AGENZIA CONTRASTO, ROME) t; **53tr** *John Coltrane* (PHOTO VAL WILMER) p; **54l** *Jimi Hendrix* (PHOTO ROBERT KNIGHT/REDFERNS, LONDON) p; **55tr** *Miles Davis* (IGDA, MILAN) p; **56tl** *Anthony Braxton* (PHOTO STORYVILLE RECORDS) p; **56c** *Steve Lacy* (PHOTO PAOLA BENSI) p; **56b** *Art Ensemble of Chicago: Famoudoudon Moye* (PHOTO JOAN HACKETT) t; **57tr** *Henry Threadgill* (PHOTO JULES ALLEN) p; **58tl** Scene from the movie *The Cotton Club* by Francis Ford Coppola (ZOETROPE/ORION/THE KOBAL COLLECTION, LONDON) p; **58tr** *Keith Jarrett* (PHOTO ELENA CARMINATI) p; **59tl** *Pat Metheny* (PHOTO GUIDO HARARI/ AGENZIA CONTRASTO, ROME) t; **60c** *Wynton Marsalis* (PHOTO ELENLA CARMLINATI) p; **60b** *Don Byron* (PHOTO ANTHONY BARBOZA) t; **61tc** *Joshua Redman* (PHOTO WEA) p; **61tr** *Steve Coleman* (PHOTO BMG) p.

COVER (FROM LEFT TO RIGHT):
1. *Bessie Smith* (ARCHIVE NORDISK) p; **2.** Original V-Disc Collection Cover (JAZZ MAGAZINE) p; **3.** Detail of a bass drum showing a jazz parade (PRIVATE COLLECTION) p; **4.** Skyline of New York City (IGDA-RIZZOLI, MILAN) p.

BACK COVER:
1. *Billie Holiday* (PHOTO WILLIAM GOTTLIEB/REDFERNS, LONDON) p.

CONTENTS

THE PROTAGONISTS

Jazz is a type of music that narrates the search for freedom. It surged in America at the turn of the century, when the descendants of African deported slaves faced the many facets of the New World's cultural life. In jazz, the many African heritages and the European musical culture of learned tradition, folk songs, and even military band music merged. It is an all-American art that developed its distinct and original language by expressing the emotions of the exiled African people. A worldwide phenomenon, the creative spark of jazz is still alive today.

♦ A GOSPEL SINGER AND ROBERT JOHNSON (1911–1938) Religious songs and the blues—two protagonists of African-American music, inspired jazz.

♦ ARRANGERS AND COMPOSERS Fletcher Henderson (1898–1952) and Jelly Roll Morton (1885–1941). Both pianists, they shaped the first jazz orchestral idiom.

♦ BENNY GOODMAN (1909–1986) Clarinetist and bandleader. He was very popular in the 1930s and 1940s.

♦ "COUNT" BASIE (1904–1984) Starting in the 1930s, he conducted a famous orchestra that was admired for its rhythm.

♦ BILLIE HOLIDAY (1915–1959) The most acclaimed jazz singer of all time. Her voice is compared to that of a saxophone.

♦ A SLAVE Slaves arrived in the United States in the eighteenth century and sang while they worked on plantations.

♦ COLEMAN HAWKINS (1901–1969) One of the greatest virtuosos of the tenor saxophone, which he introduced to jazz.

♦ LESTER YOUNG (1909–1959) First-class tenor saxophonist, he became popular in the mid-1930s.

♦ THE REVOLUTIONARIES Charlie "Bird" Parker (1920–1955) and Dizzy Gillespie (1917–1993) Saxophonist and trumpeter, respectively. By the middle of the 1940s they were the forerunners of bebop.

◆ **GLENN MILLER** (1904–1944) With his orchestra, the most celebrated Big Band during World War II, he popularized jazz in Europe.

◆ **SONNY ROLLINS** (1930–) **AND CHARLES MINGUS** (1922–1979) One of the most talented saxophonists and double-bass player-composers.

◆ **MILES DAVIS** (1926–1991) Trumpeter and composer. The constant renovation of his music reflected his restless artistic progression.

◆ **JOHN "TRANE" COLTRANE** (1926–1967) Unsurpassed master of the saxophone, his music communicated a tormented spiritual quest.

◆ **ORNETTE COLEMAN** (1930–) A talented saxophonist, he was the free jazz theoretician that shook jazz in the 1960s.

◆ **HENRY THREADGILL** (1944–) Saxophonist and composer. He is considered the heir of Ellington and Mingus.

◆ **THELONIOUS MONK** (1917–1982) Pianist, composer, and one of the most restless geniuses of jazz.

◆ **CELEBRITIES** Duke Ellington (1899–1974) and Louis Armstrong (1901–1971). The most famous orchestra leader and trumpet player in the history of jazz.

◆ **STEVE COLEMAN** (1956–) Saxophonist, composer, and one of the new names in the world of jazz.

SLAVERY

In 1619, the first Africans were brought to Virginia. At first, they were employed as servants under contract in the English colonies; later, in the middle of the seventeenth century, the slave trade grew, receiving legislative recognition at the end of the century. Slaves were sold in auctions and bought mainly by planters to cultivate cotton, sugar, and coffee. Treated as property, slaves suffered great hardships and humiliations in the New World.

♦ FROM AFRICA TO AMERICA
Slave trade with Africa had started at the end of the fifteenth century when the Portuguese went in search of laborers for their colonies in the East Indies and in the New World. The Spanish, English, French, and Dutch followed them. Unscrupulous merchants, known as slave traders, bought people who were enslaved by other Africans during intertribal wars, exchanging them for goods, then stowing them in the holds of their ships. Chained in cramped, dark spaces, with little food and water, more than twelve million Africans during four centuries were forced to leave Africa and cross the Atlantic Ocean to reach the Americas after an excruciating two-month trip. Above, a watercolor portraying a French slave trade ship at the end of the seventeenth century.

♦ AN INHUMANE TRIP
Crowded into the ship, slaves started their odyssey. At least one and a half million of them died during the agonizing trip across the ocean. Above, an engraving showing the cruelty.

♦ DRAMATIC SCENES
Slaves had no rights. A mother could be separated from her children and each one could be sold separately.

♦ **THE CIVIL WAR**
Slavery was abolished in the United States in 1865, after the Civil War (left, a painting of a battle) was won by the Northern Abolitionist States over the South.

♦ **SOLD AT AUCTION**
After a period of quarantine following the hardships of their long voyage, slaves were sold in public auctions.

♦ **THE AUCTIONEER**
Paid by the slave traders, experienced auctioneers were in charge of selling the slaves.

♦ **TEETH AND EYES**
Plantation owners carefully checked the health status of the "property," especially the teeth and the whites of the eyes, for signs of illness.

THREE CENTURIES OF AFRO-AMERICA

♦ **COTTON AND WHIPS**
Cotton (above, in a 1787 engraving of a flower) was the most widely cultivated plant in the South. Thanks to the slaves, its production constantly increased. Production jumped from 80,000 tons in 1815 to 1,150,000 tons in 1861. Since the time needed to harvest cotton fibers was short, the slaves were forced to work nights by the light of the moon. Each slave was assigned a fixed quota of cotton to pick, which was regularly checked at the end of the day by weighing each basket. If the slave's workload was underweight, he or she was whipped. The wounds were later washed with water and salt to heal painfully and serve as a warning to the other slaves. Other products grown on the plantations were rice, sugar cane, tobacco, and hemp.

Once they were bought by slave owners, the slaves were transferred to plantations or employed as house servants. In addition to large plantations, many small farms flourished in the South, where the white master often owned no more than one or two slaves. This caused the disintegration of social and family ties as well as the loss of cultural homogeneity among Africans, but it stressed contact with whites. And so a new culture was born, called African-American, which would later convey to music the complex story of the relationship between Africans and the New World.

♦ **THE WORK SONG**
Following African custom, a leader sang and the other workers sang along, trying to catch the rhythm that would soothe them in their work. On the planatations, the first African-American musical form was born: the *Work Song*.

♦ **THE BASKET**
The slave carried a sack around his or her neck that emptied into a basket. Each slave picked almost 200 pounds (91 kg) of cotton in one day.

◆ **Cotton's Road**
Once harvested, the cotton was prepared for shipment. At the end of the eighteenth century, with the first spinning machines, cotton ceased to be a luxury product.

◆ **Mansions and Shacks**
Near the master's lavish dwellings were the miserable slave quarters where the slaves were kept. Many had neither windows nor beds.

◆ **Overseers with Whips**
The landowner or his overseers, who watched over the slaves, were ready to whip the slaves for the slightest offense.

THE BLUES

The blues took shape at the end of the nineteenth century in the rural areas of the South, as a synthesis of more ancient forms of monodic or one-voice singing. Itinerant musicians, whose stage settings were village and city roads and small barrooms spread this music. The African-American blues musician expressed joys, sorrows, desires, and anxieties experienced along his road to acceptance into the white society after the abolition of slavery. The blues have an antiphonal structure, produced by alternating the voice and an impromptu musical theme.

♦ ROBERT JOHNSON (1911–1938) Guitar player and singer. He was one of the fathers of the Delta Blues, the typical blues heard around the Mississippi Delta. Between 1936 and 1937, he recorded 29 songs that have become classics. He suddenly disappeared under mysterious circumstances.

♦ THE SHACKS
African-American families lived in humble shacks in abject poverty.

♦ MUSIC AND LIFE
The blues music narrates everyday true personal experiences with realistic—and often humorous—tones.

♦ THE MUSIC
Precursor of jazz, this timeless and outstanding music continues today to renew its forms of expression. In the 1940s and 1950s, the popularity of the blues surpassed that of jazz.

♦ **THE EMPRESS OF THE BLUES** (1895–1937)
In the 1920s, the blues had an unprecedented commercial success thanks to a few female interpreters. The greatest of all is Bessie Smith, who between 1922 and 1933 sold more than two million records.

♦ **RAGTIME**
At the end of the nineteenth century, another musical style, an ancestor of jazz, flourished. It was called ragtime, a lively and rhythmic music originally composed for piano. Ragtime is formed by the two words *rag* and *time,* suggestive of the typical syncopated rhythm marked by constant acceleration. From piano music performed on perforated player piano rolls, ragtime turned into an orchestral music. Its most noteworthy representative was Scott Joplin (1868–1917), composer of the famous "Maple Leaf Rag" (above, an original sheet of music). Ragtime, also popular in Europe, inspired the first jazz piano soloists such as James P. Johnson (1894–1955), Fats Waller (1904–1943), Willie "The Lion" Smith (1897–1973), and "Jelly Roll" Morton (1885–1941).

♦ **A JUNK DEALER**
At the end of the Civil War (1865), such musical instruments as cornets, trombones, and tubas, left behind by the military brass bands of the defeated Southern army, were easy to find in the shops of any junk dealer. Even former slaves were able to buy instruments and become proficient.

LOUIS ARMSTRONG

"Satchmo" was one of the greatest jazz soloists of all time, the musician who defined some of the characteristics of jazz that remain today. Thanks to him, the solo—a series of variations executed by the musician on the melody chosen as the point of departure of the music—became the heart of the performance. The wonderful sound of his trumpet, almost an extension of his voice, was vigorous, dramatic, and uniquely magic. After him, every jazz musician would search for his own sound. Extraordinary showman, he was, above all, the world's ambassador of jazz, an artist gifted with an irresistible verve and jovial empathy, loved by his audiences.

♦ **LOUIS ARMSTRONG** (1901–1971) In his hometown, New Orleans, the young Louis Armstrong had his musical debut in a vocal quartet formed with some friends. He mastered the cornet and in the 1920s accompanied the most popular blues singers, like Bessie Smith, becoming known as a second trumpet in King Oliver's Creole Jazz Band. His hits as a soloist were composed around the middle of the 1920s with his bands, the Hot Fives and the Hot Seven, with whom he created such great successes as: "West End Blues," "Potato Head Blues," "St. James Infirmary," and "Cornet Chop Suey." His long and versatile career was marked by a steady success and lasted until the 1960s. In 1952 the readers of the music magazine *Down Beat* elected him "the most important musician of all time."

♦ **BASEBALL AND MUSIC** The favorite pastime of Louis' friends was sports. In the reform school, the young men participated in sports, played music, and were made to choose jobs.

◆ A SHOT IN STORYVILLE

In 1912 a gun was fired on New Year's Eve and eleven-year-old Louis Armstrong was sent to prison, a reform school, the Colored Waifs' Home for Boys. It is here, that his musical career began, in the Waifs' Home Brass Band.

◆ BIX BEIDERBECKE

(1903–1931) Beiderbecke had a wretched life. An outstanding cornetist, his introverted style counteracted that of Armstrong. He died young, destroyed by alcohol.

◆ A MUSIC TEACHER

Peter Davis, who directed the Waifs' Home Brass Band, gave Louis Armstrong his first music lessons. He trained him first on the tambourine, then on the saxophone, and finally on the cornet.

RHYTHM AND BLUES

During the 1940s many African-Americans moved from the rural areas of the South to the big cities of the North to work in the defense plants. Their music followed the tradition of gospel and blues songs, which, crossing paths with big band swing, created rhythm and blues. The focal point of this rhythmically swaying new music was singing, and soloists were also able to extract sounds from their instruments similar to human cries.

♦ **THE SON OF RHYTHM AND BLUES—ROCK AND ROLL**
From the blues and rhythm and blues came the sensual and energetic force that would become rock and roll, as well as a preference for a marked rhythmic pulsation and the use of the electric guitar. The term "rock and roll" can be heard in some rhythm and blues lyrics. The first American rock stars, like Elvis Presley (above) or Bill Haley, studied the sounds of the blues and rhythm and blues. Young English rock artists like the Beatles and the Rolling Stones (below, Keith Richards) did the same. Their first concern was to revive the classics of the African-American tradition.

♦ **T-BONE WALKER** (1910–1975) He was one of the most influential guitarists of the 1940s and 1950s. He was also a model for rock and roll guitarists.

♦ **RAY CHARLES**
(1932–)
A pianist, singer, and saxophonist, he emphasized the religious background of this music. A living legend of rhythm and blues, he is, along with James Brown, the forerunner of soul music.

♦ **JAMES BROWN**
(1928–)
In the heyday of rock and roll, the "Godfather of Soul" went back to the rhythmic roots of African-American music, whose sound he proudly imitated.

♦ **RHYTHM AND BLUES DANCING**
Acrobatic moves were as common among the musicians as they were among rhythm and blues dancers and audiences.

♦ **FROM THE GHETTO TO THE DOWNTOWN AREA**
People met in bars and clubs to socialize or to dance to the sound of a popular hit blaring out of the jukebox. Rhythm and blues replaced jazz, becoming the new sound of African-Americans and recording their moods and dreams.

RECORDINGS

Since 1917, when the Original Dixieland Jazz Band recorded "Livery Stable Blues," records have narrated the history of jazz. They have become the best device to capture the originality of a performance, its unique flavor dictated by the artist's spirit of the moment. Recordings have stored the historical evolution of jazz, making its legacy available to future generations. Until the 1940s, records had been issued mostly by specialized record companies, independent from the industry giants. These new small companies were able to discover and promote the development of new creative trends and were also protagonists of the history of jazz.

♦ **FROM 78S TO CDS**
Various steps and different devices trace the history of recorded jazz, from the "race records" of the 1920s, conceived exclusively for the African-American market, to the elegant compact disc reissues that today present the work of the great legends. These crucial steps were the use of an electric recording system in 1926 and the magnetic recorder, which by means of a magnetic tape allowed lengthy recordings. This explains the switch from the ten-inch (25 cm) 78 rpm record that contained only a few minutes of music, to the twelve-inch (30 cm) 33 1/3 rpm record, the long-playing (LP) record that held almost twenty minutes of music on each side. In the early 1980s, digital technology introduced, at last, the compact disc, considered time-resistant and with a clear sound.

♦ **FROM THE STUDIO TO THE RECORD STORE**
A record is made by first recording the music in the recording studio. Mixing follows with the creation of the "master," and finally the printing of copies for distribution.

♦ **TECHNICAL SUPPORT**
The producer, who assists the musicians, and the sound engineer, who records the piece, are always present in the recording studio with the musicians.

◆ THE TAKES
Every cut, even the discarded versions, is numbered in order to identify it. These numbered cuts (takes) are then assembled in compilations, which document the creative progression of the artist.

♦ **SONNY ROLLINS**
(1930–)
His career started during the bebop era alongside Charlie Parker and Bud Powell, from whom he had inherited a passion for the research of an authoritative and distinct instrumental voice. The powerful sound of his saxophone well matched his nickname of "Saxophone Colossus," which was the title of one of his records in 1956. His collaboration in the same year with trumpeter, Clifford Brown (1930–1956) lasted only few months due to Brown's premature death. Rollins went on to make some remarkable recordings such as "Tenor Madness" (1956), with his colleague, John Coltrane, and "The Freedom Suite" (1958). Rollins is still active today and is one of the most inspired geniuses of jazz, as he proved in 1985 during a concert for solo saxophone at the Museum of Modern Art in New York, which has been issued as a record.

IN SEARCH OF AN IDENTITY

By the mid-1950s West Coast Jazz, a refined style that diluted the African-American elements of this music, had triumphed. In New York, African-American musicians responded by returning to the roots of jazz—from the blues and gospel came hard bop, a tougher and cruder bop that was mastered by Sonny Rollins, Thelonious Monk, Art Blakey, and Miles Davis. This was a transitional period, during which the most typical instrumental jazz group, the quintet, featuring trumpet, saxophone, piano, double bass, and drums, predominated. The solos, the nucleus of bebop performances, became longer and longer, while arrangements became simpler.

♦ **ART BLAKEY**
(1919–1990)
One of the wildest jazz drummers, his style was directly connected to African polyrhythm. For three generations, new jazz talents emerged in his group, The Jazz Messengers.

♦ **BILL EVANS**
(1929–1980)
A white pianist admired by African-American musicians, he collaborated with Miles Davis on the masterpiece "Kind of Blue." His 1960s trio inspired the equality of the improvising roles, a crucial step in modern jazz.

♦ **A POWERFUL RESONANCE**
Rollins decided to play the saxophone nights on the Williamsburg Bridge to maximize the power of his saxophone and to be considerate to his neighbors. The experience inspired his record "The Bridge."

♦ **THELONIOUS MONK**
(1917–1982)
Although he was one of the promoters of the bebop revolution, the public ignored pianist and composer Thelonious Monk, for some time. He became known only during the second half of the 1950s, thanks to a series of important recordings in which he performed alongside saxophonists Sonny Rollins, Johnny Griffin (1928–), and Charlie Rouse (1924–1988). Monk is one of the most unpredictable central figures of jazz, an authentic mentor who underwrote several compositions, some of which have become jazz standards, thanks also to their interpretation by many jazz musicians. Among them are "Round Midnight" (1944), "Misterioso" (1948), and "Monk's Mood" (1957). A complex man, Monk was also noted for his eccentric ways, his long silences, and the unusual dances he improvised around the piano during concerts.

♦ **THE WILLIAMSBURG BRIDGE**
One of the four bridges that connect Manhattan Island to the contiguous States. It was completed in 1903, twenty years after another famous bridge, the Brooklyn Bridge. More than 240,000 people cross it every day.

ELECTRIC JAZZ

Around the mid-1960s, young people fell in love with rock. It became a hit with such new electric instruments as guitar, bass, piano, and organ. With its drive and openness, rock found its apotheosis in the enormous gatherings at Monterey, Woodstock, and the Isle of Wight, establishing itself as the sound track of an era, characterized by youth protest movements. It was the new idiom, able to overcome barriers and borders. Jazz, which was at first loved less by the general public, soon took hold of these new sounds. Miles Davis, sensitive to the spirit of the times, opened the way for the new music. And in the 1970s, many musicians blended jazz and rock music into fusion jazz.

♦ **JIMI HENDRIX**
(1942–1970) Guitarist, singer, and composer, he remains a legend today. With his music, he glorified the bursting power of rock, reinterpreting the blues tradition.

♦ **WEATHER REPORT**
Saxophonist, Wayne Shorter (1933–), and keyboardist, Joe Zawinul (1932–), who played with Miles Davis, founded the famous group, Weather Report, in 1970.

♦ **LOVE, PEACE, AND MUSIC**
Rock concerts become magical and frantic scenes. Miles Davis was among the first to desert jazz clubs and concert halls for this more spectacular arena for his music.

♦ **THE CROWD**
Under the bandstand or on their feet, exuberant young crowds enjoy the concert.

♦ **ORGANS AND KEYBOARDS**
Instead of the traditional piano, there are now new keyboards, rich in various sound effects.

♦ PLAY OF LIGHTS
AND THOUSANDS
OF WATTS
Daylight illumina-
tion, multicolor
lights, cables on
the floor, and
loud speakers
make up the
dazzling atmos-
phere of the
concert.

♦ THE
INSTRUMENTS
Typical rock music
instruments, such
as electric bass
and guitar,
found their
place in jazz.

♦ MILES DAVIS
(1926–1991)
A renowned trum-
peter, he achieved
prominence play-
ing with Charlie
Parker during the
bop years. He
went through the
various changes in
modern jazz and
was receptive to
rock's electricity.
In 1969 his record,
"Bitches Brew,"
reflected the turn-
ing point of his
musicianship. His
obscure and
visionary music
adopted some of
the sound sugges-
tions of rock at
that time. He
appreciated Jimi
Hendrix and his
explosive remake
of the blues, and
James Brown and
his messages of
African-American
assertiveness.
Miles was influ-
enced by them
and elaborated on
a type of music
based on complex
rhythmic textures
and electric
sounds not heard
before in jazz.
Soon, his col-
leagues, who cre-
ated their own
groups, followed
his influence.
Among them were
the Mahavishnu
Orchestra, direct-
ed by guitarist
John McLaughlin
(1942–), and the
Headhunters,
directed by pianist
Herbie Hancock
(1940–).

JAZZ IN THE WORLD

♦ **MOVIES AND JAZZ**
The youngest of the forms of art and jazz have often come together. Films can offer a wide retrospective in images of the African-American musical evolution. The "soundies" of the 1930s, predecessors of videoclips, are short movies that present the cut live on the screen. Among the protagonists of soundies are: Louie Armstrong, Duke Ellington, Cab Calloway, and Billie Holiday. The documentary cinema is more detailed in its historical reporting of interviews, anecdotes, and performances. Jazz has also enhanced film narratives of the biographies of musicians with sound tracks. Among the well-known movies on jazz are: *The Cotton Club* (1984) by Francis Ford Coppola (above, a scene), *'Round Midnight* (1984) by Bertrand Tavernier, and *Bird* (1988) directed by Clint Eastwood, about the life and music of Charlie Parker.

Since the 1920s and the arrival of American musicians in Europe, jazz has been exported beyond the American shores. Its popularity has increased over the years through records, magazines, books, and movies, which, along with festivals and concerts, convinced musicians in other countries to follow the example of the Americans. Today, jazz is a universal idiom, popular everywhere in the world. One of the influences that has greatly contributed to its expansion is education. The oral tradition, typical of the beginning of jazz, has been replaced by a complex system of schools, where the works of the legends of jazz are analyzed and studied by students and professors.

♦ **KEITH JARRETT**
(1945–)
One of today's finest pianists still at work, he has helped to bring the world of jazz closer to classical music, from the music of Miles Davis to that of Johann Sebastian Bach.

♦ **LEARNING RHYTHM AT SCHOOL**
Those who take drum lessons get some exercise using pens and pencils as drumsticks.

♦ **A MUSICIAN FOR A TEACHER**
Musicians often teach their own techniques to students.

♦ **NOTES AND SWING**
Two beats for drums are written on the blackboard. Notations underline every rhythmic accent.

♦ **ACCENTS AND RHYTHMS**
A student practices on drums what the teacher is explaining.

♦ **PAT METHENY**
(1954–)
Virtuoso of the guitar, he is the promoter of a synthesis between jazz, rock, and other ethnic sounds.

♦ **JAZZ IN SCHOOLS**
In public and private schools, as well as in prestigious conservatories, it is possible to study jazz, practice an instrument or learn composition or arranging.

INDEX